First World War
and Army of Occupation
War Diary
France, Belgium and Germany

1 INDIAN CAVALRY DIVISION
Lucknow Cavalry Brigade
Machine Gun Squadron
12 January 1916 - 31 December 1916

WO95/1175/4

The Naval & Military Press Ltd
www.nmarchive.com
Published in association with The National Archives

Published by

The Naval & Military Press Ltd

Unit 10 Ridgewood Industrial Park,

Uckfield, East Sussex,

TN22 5QE England

Tel: +44 (0) 1825 749494

www.naval-military-press.com

www.nmarchive.com

This diary has been reprinted in facsimile from the original. Any imperfections are inevitably reproduced and the quality may fall short of modern type and cartographic standards.

© **Crown Copyright**
Images reproduced by permission of The National Archives, London, England, 2015.

Contents

Document type	Place/Title	Date From	Date To
Heading	WO95/1175/4		
Heading	BEF 1 Ind. Cav. Div. Lucknow Bde. Machine Gun Sqd. 1916 Jan to 1916 Dec		
Heading	War Diary of Lucknow Machine Gun Squadron From 31st January 1916 To 29th February 1916		
War Diary	Quesnoy-Le-Montant	31/01/1916	07/02/1916
War Diary	Miannay	08/02/1916	08/02/1916
War Diary	Cahon	10/02/1916	10/02/1916
War Diary	Frieres	12/01/1916	12/01/1916
War Diary	Quesnoy-Le-Montant	14/02/1916	16/02/1916
War Diary	Gouey	17/02/1916	17/02/1916
War Diary	Quesnoy-Le-Montant	19/02/1916	19/02/1916
War Diary	Mons	20/02/1916	20/02/1916
War Diary	Quesnoy Le-Montant	21/02/1916	28/02/1916
Heading	War Diary of Machine. Gun Squadron Lucknow Cavalry Brigade From 1st March 19116 To 30 April 1916.		
War Diary	Quesnoy-Le-Montant	01/03/1916	13/03/1916
War Diary	Cayeux	14/03/1916	14/03/1916
War Diary	Quesnoy-Le-Montant	15/03/1916	16/03/1916
War Diary	Monchy	17/03/1916	17/03/1916
War Diary	Quesnoy Le Montant	18/03/1916	26/03/1916
War Diary	Caumont	26/03/1916	09/04/1916
War Diary	Genappes	10/04/1916	15/04/1916
War Diary	Caumont	16/04/1916	30/04/1916
Heading	War Diary of Machine Gun Squadron, Lucknow Cavalry Brigade From 1st May 196 To 31st May 1916.		
War Diary	Caumont	01/05/1916	03/05/1916
War Diary	Le Festel	04/05/1916	06/05/1916
War Diary	Caumont	07/05/1916	15/05/1916
War Diary	Honval	16/05/1916	17/06/1916
Heading	War Diary of Machine Gun Squadron Lucknow Cavalry Brigade From 1st July 1916 To 31st July 1916		
War Diary	La Folie Farm	01/07/1916	01/07/1916
War Diary	Near Lucheux	01/07/1916	01/07/1916
War Diary	Frohen-Le-petit	02/07/1916	18/07/1916
War Diary	Bethencourt	19/07/1916	31/07/1916
Heading	War Diary of Machine Gun Squadron, Lucknow Cavalry Brigade. From 1st August 1916 To 31st August		
War Diary	Bethencourt	01/08/1916	09/08/1916
War Diary	Humbercourt	09/08/1916	31/08/1916
Heading	War Diary of Machine Gun Squadron Lucknow Cavalry Brigade From 1st September 1916 To 30th September 1916		
War Diary	Humbercourt	01/09/1916	02/09/1916
War Diary	Occoches	03/09/1916	03/09/1916
War Diary	Brailly	04/09/1916	10/09/1916
War Diary	Frohen-Le Petit	11/09/1916	11/09/1916
War Diary	Grouches	12/09/1916	12/09/1916
War Diary	Querrieux	13/09/1916	14/09/1916

War Diary	Dernancourt	15/09/1916	26/09/1916
Miscellaneous	Mametz Bussy-les-Dours	27/09/1916	27/09/1916
War Diary	Hangest	28/09/1916	28/09/1916
War Diary	Eaucourt Sur-Somme	29/09/1916	29/09/1916
War Diary	Crecy	30/09/1916	30/09/1916
Heading	War Diary of Machine Gun Squadron, Lucknow Cavalry Brigade From 1st October 1916 To 30th November		
War Diary	Crecy	01/10/1916	06/10/1916
War Diary	Buigny	07/10/1916	07/10/1916
War Diary	Crecy	08/10/1916	21/10/1916
War Diary	Sailly au Bois	22/10/1916	22/10/1916
War Diary	Hebuterne	23/10/1916	15/11/1916
War Diary	Betrancourt	16/11/1916	19/11/1916
War Diary	Betrancourt (advanced Hdqrs of L.M.G.S. ? of 6th Ave & View. Trench	19/11/1916	20/11/1916
War Diary	6th Ave & Virix Trench	21/11/1916	21/11/1916
War Diary	Bertrencourt	21/11/1916	25/11/1916
War Diary	En ronte to Woincourt.	26/11/1916	26/11/1916
Miscellaneous	Hymmeville	27/11/1916	30/11/1916
Heading	War Diary of Machine Gun Squadron Lucknow Cavalry Brigade From 1st December 1916 To 31st December 1916.		
Heading	War Diary of Machine Gun Squadron For the month of December, 1916.		
War Diary	Hymmeville	01/12/1916	31/12/1916

WO 95/1175/4 Sb OM

BEF
1 IND. CAV. DIV.

LUCKNOW BDE.

MACHINE GUN SQD.

1916 JAN to 1916 DEC

SERIAL No. 316.

Confidential

War Diary

of

Lucknow Machine Gun Squadron

FROM 31st January 1916 TO 29th February 1916

Army Form C. 2118.

WAR DIARY
of
INTELLIGENCE SUMMARY. LUCKNOW. MACHINE. GUN. SQUADRON.

(Erase heading not required.)

Instructions regarding War Diaries and Intelligence Summaries are contained in F. S. Regs. Part II. and the Staff Manual respectively. Title pages will be prepared in manuscript.

Place	Date	Hour	Summary of Events and Information	Remarks and references to Appendices
QUESNOY-LE-MONTANT	1915 JAN. 31st		The LUCKNOW MACHINE GUN SQUADRON formed, and concentrated in the Sugar Refinery at QUESNOY-LE-MONTANT according to the War Establishment for a M.G. Squadron.* The Squadron consisted of 3 sections (of 4 guns each). The 3 sections were composed as opposite:— 4 guns from the 1st K.D. Guards, 4 " " " 29th Lancers, 4 " " " 36th Jacob's Horse. Total 12 " The Officers appointed to the Squadron were as under:— Capt. M.M. Carpendale, 36th Jacob's Horse — — — Commandant Capt. Z.G. Barmister, 31st Lancers att'd 29th Lancers — 2nd in Command. Lieut. B.M. Ward, 1st K.D. Guards do do Sergt. B.G. Holt, " " " " Lieut. S.A.A. Mercer, att'd 29th Lancers Risaldar Kabul Singh, 31st Lancers att'd 29th Lancers Temp. Capt. J. Graves, att'd 36th Jacob's Horse Jemadar Marbut Shah, 36th Jacob's Horse The Transport for the Squadron – pending the arrival of that laid down in the New War Establishment – consisted of 2 G.S. Wagons, and 3½ hooded wagons lent by the respective Regiments until the authorised Transport were ready to be taken over.	* forwarded under Bde. Major No 202 of 31.1.16 * Trade Bdn. Routine order No 382 of 11/2/16

3353 Wt. W3544/1454 700,000 5/15 D.D. & L. A.D.S.S./Forms/C. 2118.

Army Form C. 2118.

WAR DIARY
of
INTELLIGENCE SUMMARY. LUCKNOW MACHINE GUN SQUADRON.

(Erase heading not required.)

Place	Date	Hour	Summary of Events and Information	Remarks and references to Appendices
Quesnoy-le-Montant	1916 Feb 1st		The McConnel Pattern Equipment recently issued to all the Machine Gun Detachments was found to be most unsatisfactory, and absolutely unserviceable for any hard work. The material was made of most inferior stuff — the gun keeps on an erosive turn, & dropped the gun on the ground — the spring hooks were constantly breaking, & there was no arrangement to prevent seams from getting into the belt loops. This equipment was undoubtedly lighter, but not nearly so serviceable as the old I.P. Equipment.	
	7th	10 a.m.	Inspection of the M.G. Squadron at Irles by Br. Genl. W.H. Fasken, C.B. Comdg Lucknow Cav. Bde. The Squadron drilled exactly as a Cavalry Regt. on parade, according to plans made out by the O.C.M.G. Sqdt. Each Section of 4 guns was the same as a Sqdt., & each gun-team as a Troop. No words of command except those laid down for the drill of a Cavalry Regt. were used. The object in drilling as a Cav. Regt. was to enable the Squadron, when manoeuvring with the Brigade, to adopt exactly the same formations as a Regt. in order to conceal its identity from hostile observers. The only modifications in the drill that had to be made were that :- (a) When a Troop was on line the gun had to be on the right in front. (b) " " " " " (c) When forming Squadron from Squadron Column, the 4th Troop had to move	

Army Form C. 2118.

WAR DIARY
of
INTELLIGENCE SUMMARY. LUCKNOW MACHINE GUN SQUADRON

(Erase heading not required.)

Place	Date	Hour	Summary of Events and Information	Remarks and references to Appendices
QUESNOY-LE-MONTANT	1916 Feb. 7		(Continued) up on the right infront of on the left, so as not to separate the 2 guns of a section.	
MIANNAY.	8:	10 A.M.	Tactical Exercise for the K.D.G M. Guns. The chief points brought were these:— (i) The disadvantages in separating your guns unnecessarily, & the difficulties in keeping up communication & controlling the fire of your guns when widely separated. (ii) The necessity for some proper "Squadron" to replenish the supply of ammunition. (iii) The danger in posting your guns near distinctive landmarks.	
CAHON.	10:	10 A.M.	Tactical Exercise for the 29th M.Guns. The lessons learnt were these:— (i) The necessity for careful range-taking by your Range takers, & the difficulty in accurately estimating ranges by eye in undulating country. (ii) That practice is essential in posting guns to cover a frontage rather wider than that normally held by M Guns.	
FRIÈRES.	12:	10 A.M.	Tactical Exercise for 36th M.Guns. The following points were noticed:— (i) The need for alternative emplacements ready prepared - in almost every position as no M. direct — or indirect, holds attack fire from an unexpected direction. (ii) The importance of every man knowing exactly what he has got to do when suddenly ordered to come into action — so that no time may be lost in doing so.	

Army Form C. 2118.

WAR DIARY
or
INTELLIGENCE SUMMARY. LUCKNOW. MACHINE GUN. SQUADRON.
(Erase heading not required.)

Place	Date 1916	Hour	Summary of Events and Information	Remarks and references to Appendices
Avesnes le Moutier F.	Feb. 14th	10 A.M	Scouted Inspection by Br. Gen. Parker C.B. Commdt Indian Cav. Bde. of the M.G. Squadron at Drill and Coming into Action. The following points were remarked on :— (1) Pace not even, & at times very much too fast (2) Too much talking by Indian Ranks when coming into action. (3) "Fire Orders" - repeated by Indian Ranks – not crisp enough – to move Reserve in giving them destination. (4) "Lead horses" too close to the Guns, & verges not taken away. In a front where good cover was obtainable.	
"	15th	1 P.M.	Three M. Guns & their Equipment have been sent from the M.G. School at NESLE NORMANDEUSE, where they were originally kept, for instructional Purposes.	
"	16th		New War Establishment received. Is different from the Provisional War Establmt. Issued on 31.1.16 as under :— (a) 2nd in Command ─ ─ ─ ─ ─ ─ ─ abolished (b) Two Indian Officers (with 29° & 36° M.Guns) ─ ─ do (c) 1 Saddler + 1 Shoeing Smith ─ ─ ─ ─ ─ do (d) 1 G.S. Wagon ─ ─ ─ ─ ─ ─ ─ ─ ─ ─ do The detail was arranged by Sections of 2 guns each instead of by Sections of 4 guns each – as provided in the 1st (Provisional) War Estab: and 1 Subaltern Officer was detailed to command each Section of 2 guns.	Indian Establ. No 234 d/6/2/16.

Army Form C. 2118.

Instructions regarding War Diaries and Intelligence Summaries are contained in F.S. Regs., Part II. and the Staff Manual respectively. Title pages will be prepared in manuscript.

WAR DIARY or INTELLIGENCE SUMMARY.

LUCKNOW. MACHINE GUN SQUADRON

(Erase heading not required.)

Place	Date 1916	Hour	Summary of Events and Information	Remarks and references to Appendices
QUESNOY le Montant	Feb 16		(Continued) Whether British or Indian. One Indian Officer was appointed (surplus to the Establishment) as attached to the M.G. Squadron under the orders of the G.O.C. Bde. Resaldar Kabul Singh, 31st Lancers att.d 29th Lancers was given the appointment.	
GOUY	17"	10.AM	"Defence of Billets" Scheme by the G.O.C. 1 Cav. Bde. With regard to the M.Guns in this scheme, the following points were remarked on:— (1) That "plunging fire" from a house for night-firing does not produce nearly so much fire effect as grazing fire would do. (2) That C.O's — Masters of Choosing the M.G. positions themselves — should point out to their M.G.O's the ground they want covered by M.G. fire, & allow their M.G.'s — in most cases — to choose their own gun positions. (3) The advantage in creating "Dummy" barricades to be fired on by M.Guns when occupied by the enemy.	
QUESNOY le Montant	19"		Capt. Z.G. Burnside 31st Lancers att.d 29th Lancers, & Jem. Machil Singh, 36" Jacobs Horse are struck off the strength of the Squadron.	1st note New War Estabt of 18/2/16
MDDIS	20"		Tactical Exercise under G.O.C. Bde. The M.G. Squadron on finding that enemy holding a wood were detailed 15 gun teams to his	

#353 Wt.W3544/1454 700,000 5/15 D.D.& L. A.D.S.S./Forms/C.2118.

Army Form C. 2118.

WAR DIARY

INTELLIGENCE SUMMARY. LUCKNOW MACHINE GUN SQUADRON

(Erase heading not required.)

Instructions regarding War Diaries and Intelligence Summaries are contained in F. S. Regs., Part II and the Staff Manual respectively. Title pages will be prepared in manuscript.

Place	Date	Hour	Summary of Events and Information	Remarks and references to Appendices
MONS	FEB. 20	10AM	(Cont'd) position, while the Lucknow Cav. Bde. moved round his flanks. The advantages in "oblique" & "enfilade" fire from this manner were well illustrated.	
QUESNOY-le-Montaul	21"		The following Transport* authorized in the New War Establish'ts arrived from ABBEVILLE :— 1. G.S. Wagon 6 G.S. limbered (double) wagons } + 32 light draught horses. 2 Water Carts	
"	22nd		Lieut. F.B. Maltby att'd 36 Jacobs Horse on return from leave joins from M.G. Sqr. Drivers for the above Transport* were indented for from Reg'ts as under :—	
"	23"		7 Drivers Drawn from 1st K.D.G's. 5 Indian from 29" Lcrs. 6 Indian from 36 J.H.	
"	24.		Snow . Storm	
"	25		6 inches of snow on ground. M. guns ; owing to oil & water being frozen, would fire .	
"	26		Having added 50% of glycerine to the water & 50% of clear paraffin to the oil, the M. guns continue to fire without any interruption.	
"	27.		Thaw sets in.	
"	28		52 boxes S.A.A + 2 boxes revolver ammunition received from D.A.D.O.S. to complete reserve amm't as authorized for the M.G. Sqr. in the new War Establishments	

1577 Wt. W10791/1773 500,000 1/15 D. D. & L. A.D.S.S./Forms/C. 2118.

SERIAL NO. 316.

Confidential
War Diary

of

Machine Gun Squadron, Lucknow Cavalry Brigade.

FROM 1st March, 1916 TO 30th April, 1916.

Army Form C. 2118.

WAR DIARY
of LUCKNOW. M. GUN. SQUADRON.
INTELLIGENCE SUMMARY.

(Erase heading not required.)

Instructions regarding War Diaries and Intelligence Summaries are contained in F. S. Regs., Part II. and the Staff Manual respectively. Title pages will be prepared in manuscript.

Place	Date	Hour	Summary of Events and Information	Remarks and references to Appendices
QUESNOY Le-Montant	1916 March 1st	10.A.M.	Squadron Drill with limbers. From the movements carried out on parade, it is evident that (a) the horses in the limbers must be perfectly trained. (b) the drivers must have constant practice in driving under really good N.C.O's. (c) the N.C.O. i/c each limber must be an intelligent man, with some knowledge of how to find his way about the country north the aid of a map. This is important, for in action the N.C.O. will be responsible for having his limber in the position indicated. (d) Every N.C.O. knows exactly his proper position in the various formations, & understands how to get there. (e) Every driver be fairly trained in ball filling, for in action the drivers will have to do most of the best. filling worn under the supervision of the N.C.O. (f) careful fitting of saddlery, & greasing of limber wheels etc	

Army Form C. 2118.

WAR DIARY
or
INTELLIGENCE SUMMARY.
(Erase heading not required.)

Instructions regarding War Diaries and Intelligence Summaries are contained in F. S. Regs., Part II. and the Staff Manual respectively. Title pages will be prepared in manuscript.

Place	Date	Hour	Summary of Events and Information	Remarks and references to Appendices
QUESNOY-le-Montant	1916 March 2nd	4 P.M.	Brigade Tactical Scheme to illustrate the transfer of the Bde from its day positions to its held at night, when in close touch with the enemy. Points brought out were as follows :- (a) the necessity for close communication by telephone with the Bde. H.Q. & the various Regts. (b) the need for an escort to the guns when isolated.	
"	3rd	10 A.M.	Squadron Drill with limbers - together Manoeuvre. (a) The N.C.O. detailed with each limbered wagon should be the next senior to the Section Commander, so that he may be out of the danger zone, & ready to take command of the Section should the Section Commander become a Casualty. Some Officers prefer to keep their senior N.C.O.s with the guns, & hence on ordinary parade win the limber wagon. This is most incorrect, & should not be permitted. (b) Except in the line of march, when all 6 limber wagons would march in rear of the Column it is very advisable when necessary to detail an officer or senior N.C.O. to command them.	
"	4th	11 A.M.	Squadron parades with all Transports fully loaded for Route March. The following points were noted :- (a) That 1 G.S. Wagon is not sufficient	

Army Form C. 2118.

WAR DIARY or INTELLIGENCE SUMMARY.

(Erase heading not required.)

Instructions regarding War Diaries and Intelligence Summaries are contained in F.S. Regs., Part II. and the Staff Manual respectively. Title pages will be prepared in manuscript.

Place	Date	Hour	Summary of Events and Information	Remarks and references to Appendices
BUSNOY-le Montant	1916 March 4th	11.A.M	to carry the kits of 7 P.O. 210 centre/pk (Brit. & Indian). and also Med. Kit & cookery pots, Farriers, Saddlers, & Medical kit, Officers kit & surplus stores etc. on hand. (b) the necessity for spare change of horses to replace those lame or unfit for work. (c) the urgency & advisability of having broken wagons sent to Ordnance workshops at once for repair. (d) The importance of every officer & N.C.O. knowing exactly what ammunition etc. has to be put on the double-limber'd wagons, & knowing how to pack it. All Transport drivers are pleased at disposal of Bn's Transport Officer for instruction in harness fitting - driving etc every day at 2.30 P.M. Sergeant ADDISON to be appointed S.Q.M.S. vice S.Q.M.S. Pierce returned to 'A' Sqdn R.D.G.s. Snow & weather very cold. - Ground very damp & unfit for working over. Confidential Memo * received abolishing the British & Indian Cav. Corps	* B.M No O.5/02.16 2/26/2/16 I/Divt. Cav Corps

WAR DIARY
INTELLIGENCE SUMMARY
(Erase heading not required.)

Army Form C. 2118.

Place	Date	Hour	Summary of Events and Information	Remarks and references to Appendices
AVESNES Le Comte	1916 March 4th	—	(Cont'd) and allotting as Reserve the Divisions as under :—	
			1st Cav. Div. to 1st Army	
			2nd Cav. Div. " 2nd "	
			1st Ind. Cav. Div. " 3rd "	
			2nd " " " " 4th "	
			The 3rd Cav. Div. & Canadian Cavalry Bde. to form a Reserve under G.H.Q.	
"	5th	10 A.M.	Brade inspection was was with all Transport, Guns, horses.	
"	6th	—	Weather very cold — snow & rain.	
"	7th	—	Very hard frost during night.	
		10.45 A.M.	Inspection of M.G. Squadron near FRIEVILLES by G.O.C. 1st Indian Cav. Division/Major Gen. the paid particular attention to the fitting & loading of equipment (to the Indian C.B.) Maconochie pattern in particular, which he condemned & ordered to the next issue) and to the Transport of the Squadron.	
"	9th	10 A.M.	Polo Tactical Exercise under G.O.C. Bde. near ST. VALERY. The question arose as to whether a M. Gun Section attached to a Squadron should be under the orders of the O.C. Squadron, or the O.C. M.G. Section or Sections, and it was decided	

Army Form C. 2118.

WAR DIARY
or
INTELLIGENCE SUMMARY
(Erase heading not required.)

Instructions regarding War Diaries and Intelligence Summaries are contained in F. S. Regs., Part II. and the Staff Manual respectively. Title Pages will be prepared in manuscript.

Place	Date	Hour	Summary of Events and Information	Remarks and references to Appendices
QUESNOY-LE-Montant	March 9th	10 A.M	(Continued) That (a) The M.G Section attached should be under the orders of the O.C Squadron. (b) The O.C Squadron should point out to the O.C M.G. Section the front & special objects that he wanted M.G. fire to be brought on to. And the approximate line to be held by his Squadron — but that he should leave the choice of gun positions to the O.C M.G. Section. (c) Having chosen his gun positions the O.C M.G. Section should get into touch with the guns on his right & left, & arrange to sweep with cross-fire the ground in front of the Squadrons on either flank. He would do this by the preparation of altitude aeroplane mounts, so as to be prepared for an attack from an unexpected quarter. Weather - cold but dry. In afternoon had Car Sports at CHEPY - Results as under:- Tug- of- War. 38th Jacobs Horse beat 38th C.I.H (5 minutes pull). Wrestling on horses - 2nd Lancers beat 19th Lancers.	
"	10th		Hard frost & some snow	
"	13th	10 P.M	Squadron Drill without linked horses. The necessity for all Officers having more practice in shutting in a fast pace were brought out	

Army Form C. 2118.

WAR DIARY
or
INTELLIGENCE SUMMARY
(Erase heading not required.)

Place	Date	Hour	Summary of Events and Information	Remarks and references to Appendices
CAYEUX	March 14	10 AM	The Division on Reli rendezvoused at 10 A.M. & marched to the seashore near NEW BRIGHTON, where Brigade Drill from Tactical Manoeuvres took place. The R.A. drilled without the M.G. Squadron, but on carrying out a mounted attack & a pursuit, The M. Guns were called into operation and acted out as per diagram below:—	

WAR DIARY or INTELLIGENCE SUMMARY

Army Form C. 2118.

Place	Date	Hour	Summary of Events and Information	Remarks and references to Appendices
CAYEUX	Mar 14	10 A.M.	(Cont'd) The Bde was to attack the enemy at X; "W" Battery was to take up a position so as to cover the Bde whilst getting up to the point of deployment, & to continue firing till the last moment before the Brigade charged home. The M.G. Squadron started to head of the Bde - then drew up to the senior flank, & dropped the M.G guns, by 2 at a time which immediately came into action, & opened fire on the objective. This was carried out correctly, & the M.Guns were not at any time within the Bde when displaying for the attack. The orders for the pursuit were :- { N.Bde + 29 + 7cm + 1 section R. Artillery + 1 group of M.Guns to pursue { 36th J.M + 2 sections R. Artillery + 2 groups of M.Guns to be in reserve.	
QUESNOY-LE-Montant	15 } 16 }		Weather fine & dry.	
MONCHY	17		Divisional Tactical Exercise near MONCHY. - Illustrating the tactical handling of a Cavalry Bde in a retirement when opposed by superior numbers. As regards M guns it was considered advisable to have as many as possible with them party of the rear guard, & to keep sections with - as far as possible so as to facilitate the withdrawal of them to the next position.	

Army Form C. 2118.

WAR DIARY
or
INTELLIGENCE SUMMARY

(Erase heading not required.)

Instructions regarding War Diaries and Intelligence Summaries are contained in F. S. Regs., Part II. and the Staff Manual respectively. Title Pages will be prepared in manuscript.

Place	Date	Hour	Summary of Events and Information	Remarks and references to Appendices
AVESNOT le Mesnil	18		Weather fine - no rain	
	19			
	20			
	21		Inspection of horses by O.C. M.V.S. He considered the grazing of horses for 1/2 hour daily to be necessary in order to improve the horses coats.	
	22		Weather wet again with rain	
	23		18 dismounted men marched from 1st Rgt to be attached to the M4 Squadron for duty. Instead of asking for reinforcements from Rgt on casualties men - in future the Squadron will be reinforced from twice dismounted men, their places being filled up by dismounting from the Base depot.	
	24		Two G.S. Wagons sent from the Auxiliary Horse Transport to carry the tents & extra kit of the Squadron to the new billeting area. March order parade with loaded transport (rehearsal) March orders for 25th (to new billeting area) cancelled	
	25		Stood fast awaiting orders to move to new billeting area.	
	26		Cold wind & rain till noon. Squadron marched at 8am to GOUY watered in Somme Canal, arrived rendezvous S. exit of BONNEVALLE 10am, march in rear of 29 Lancers via CANCHY, watered & fed (1pm) le BOISLE 4, weather having cleared, halted till 2.15pm. Arrived 3.30pm at new billets CAUMONT.	
CAUMONT				

Army Form C. 2118.

WAR DIARY
or
INTELLIGENCE SUMMARY
(Erase heading not required.)

Place	Date 1916 MARCH	Hour	Summary of Events and Information	Remarks and references to Appendices
CAUMONT	26		'A' echelon arrived 4 p.m. 'B' echelon & all details arrived by 6.30 p.m. Horses picketed in open, 36th & 29th on Rt bank of FONTAINE RIANTE stream, K.D.G's in an orchard. Heavy showers at intervals turned the standings into a morass. All horses stood the march well.	
"	27		Horses exercised & grazed, arms & machine guns inspected, day spent in cleaning up.	
"	28		Arranged, in company with Interpreter Brown the Maire's stabling under cover in anticipation of severe weather to move into stables. Started cleaning up stables to be ready for Disinfection. The Interpreter took notes of existing damage to stables (attributable to French Cavalry) in view of possible damage claims hereafter. — The Maire was present throughout. Capt Carpendale hunts proceeded on leave, command of Sqn devolves on Gilfinians. Fine.	
"	29		Inspection by Lt. Gen. Fasken C in C. New Brigade of billets, horse lines and proposed stabling. Gen. Fasken expressed satisfaction but laid stress on the following points. (1) Indoor rounds must be made accustomed to the tidy habits in regard to bedding & equipment, inculcated upon with British rounds in barracks. (2) great attention must be paid to the proper fastening of roller bands. Breast straps & number cords of filools or horses picketed in the open. (3) provision of sufficient water in the dry months of the year.	
"	30 31		} Fine, sunny.	
April	1		Fine, sunny. 1 Officer pr Group (Lt Ward K.D.G's, Lt Mercer 29th Lrs, Lt Woolly 36 S.H.) proceeded on Advanced Reconnaissance in the neighbourhood of ARRAS. They returned p.m. 4.4.16.	

Army Form C. 2118.

WAR DIARY
or
INTELLIGENCE SUMMARY
(Erase heading not required.)

Instructions regarding War Diaries and Intelligence Summaries are contained in F. S. Regs., Part II. and the Staff Manual respectively. Title Pages will be prepared in manuscript.

Place	Date 1916 APRIL	Hour	Summary of Events and Information	Remarks and references to Appendices
CAUMONT	3		Tactical exercise with 29th & 36th Groups between FONTAINE L'ETALON & CAUMONT. K.D.G. Group = Musketry.	
	4		K.D.G. Group practised concealment of guns in Buildings & choosing gun positions.	
	5		"	
	6		Dull cold dry day. A Board of Survey on Winter Clothing was held. President Capt Groves. Members — Lt Buggewitter FADOS & Lt Hall. 32 Blankets G.S. 4.16 Rugs-Large were condemned.	
			Received orders to march on 9.4.16 to training area for one week.	
	7/8		Squadron moves out of permanent billets at CAUMONT, & marches to GENAPPES for a week's Brigade Training.	
	9		Weather fine & dry. Capt Capenall returns from leave & takes over command of the Squadron.	
GENAPPES	10	9 A.M	Weather — fine & dry. Squadron Training :— to some drill movements across country with hunters and a field :— (a) hunters can go across hurdles & over practically any country with Squadron provided ground is fairly dry (b) the best formation for M. Guns or pack going across country is "line of Troops between."	
	11.	9 A.M	Weather — heavy rain Squadron Training — practice bringing m. guns into action with	

Army Form C. 2118.

WAR DIARY
INTELLIGENCE SUMMARY
(Erase heading not required.)

Instructions regarding War Diaries and Intelligence Summaries are contained in F. S. Regs., Part II. and the Staff Manual respectively. Title Pages will be prepared in manuscript.

Place	Date	Hour	Summary of Events and Information	Remarks and references to Appendices
GENAPPES	11		(Cont'd) Procedure is follows.	
		9 A.M.	(a) O.C. Squadron accompanied by the D.S.C. Groups along with their Range takers gallop to position from where the Target can be observed - alights 2½' in. firmament 'Enemy along the guns.	
			(b) O.C. Squadron Points out task to the D.S.C. Groups, who rode with their range takers to their own pace of ground, choose their gun positions & then drops their Range takers there to take the range to the Target.	
			(c) D.S.C. Groups then ride back, meet their guns, & bring them up in suitable formations to the gun positions previously chosen - at the same time pointing out to them 2.5 in. Covernment where they want their let horses taken to.	
			(d) Under orders given by his C groups, the O.C. Squadron gives the order "Drop your limbers" - on which Group commanders act just then ordering them to halt under cover. Eradlebu to the M.C.D.s. y/c limbers should Ridden be under 1000 yards from the M.G. positions.	
			(e) The position of the limbers should Ridden be under 1000 yards from the M.G. positions.	
		2 P.M.	The Brigade moved across a valley, & made a dismounted attack on infantry in the neighbourhood of the village, to MILLENCOURT. For this Scheme the M.G. guns were attached to their own units, & the following points were noticed :-	
			(a) The M.G. Squadron being a powerful reserve of fire in the hands of the Brigadier - should not be split up, & attached to Regiments	

WAR DIARY or INTELLIGENCE SUMMARY

Army Form C. 2118.

Place	Date	Hour	Summary of Events and Information	Remarks and references to Appendices
GENAPPES	11	2.P.M.	(Cont^d.) indiscriminately, but given a separate task under the O.C. Squadron by which means the fire effect would be greatly increased. It should form a sort of intermediary between the artillery & the attacking troops. (b) A M.G. Group attached to a Reg^t when moving mounted across the open to its fire position must be treated as a 5th Squadron, & adopt exactly the same formation as the Reg^t - preferably on a flank - otherwise its position is certain to be spotted - for instance :— (i) On Reg^t moving in "line of Squadron Columns" has its M.guns in "line of Troop Columns" following along in rear. (ii) Another Reg^t also in "line of Squadron Columns" but its M.guns in "Squadron Column" following the 2nd Squadron, would made the 2nd Squadron appear double the size of the other Squadrons. The above two instances should be considered from a hostile observer's point of view. (c) The M.guns were carried along with the dismounted troops in the attack. The latter advanced by rushes, with the result that as soon as a M.gun was properly land & in action, its fire was immediately smothered by the rifle fire. Weather very wet.	
"	12th	11.A.M.	The Brigade attack Infantry & guns mounted. The M.G. Squadron	

Army Form C. 2118.

WAR DIARY
INTELLIGENCE SUMMARY
(Erase heading not required.)

Instructions regarding War Diaries and Intelligence Summaries are contained in F.S. Regs., Part II. and the Staff Manual respectively. Title Pages will be prepared in manuscript.

19

Place	Date	Hour	Summary of Events and Information	Remarks and references to Appendices
GENAPPES	12.	11 P.M.	(Cont.) to this occasion was given the task of getting out to a flank, & bringing fire to bear on the enemy before the Cav. charged home. This was an example of getting into action quickly, but owing to the very heavy state of the ground a very difficult task to carry out effectually. Note :- An escort should be dismounted in a case such as this.	
"	13	9 A.M.	Weather Showery. Tactical Exercise with Ball Ammunition. The M. Guns for this Scheme were attached to their own Units, & each C.O. handled them in a different way! This was another good example of the mistake in splitting up the M.G. Squadron, & allowing the guns to have more units, — for by so doing (a) The G.O.C. loses the enormous reserve of fire he ought to have in his hands for a special task on opportunity. (b) The effect of the fire of the M Guns is very much reduced. (c) The M. Guns are not handled at their best, for C.Os. have very varied ideas as to how to use them.	
	16.	9 A.M.	The firing of all the M. Guns on this occasion was undoubtedly very good. Weather fine but cold. Squadron training cont. 2nd in Command absent from groups. Mem: Leave necessary in M.G. Sqdt. Drill for all the 2nd in Command.	

WAR DIARY
INTELLIGENCE SUMMARY

Army Form C. 2118.

Place	Date	Hour	Summary of Events and Information	Remarks, and references to Appendices
GENAPPES.	14.	11.A.M	**Flammenwerfer Demonstration.** The Machine used was the captured from the Germans at HOOGE. It was carried along by two men immediately in front of the attacking Infantry up to about 15-20 yds from the trenches. The Infantry usually rushed home their attack immediately after the flames had ceased. To caught the enemy at a decided disadvantage. The flames go upwards as there is little to fear of men in the trenches keep well down. The heat by means of meeting an attack of this kind was by M.G. fire from the flanks. The liquid consisted of a mixture of petrol, paraffin, & lubricating oil. There is no doubt that a liquid fire attack - especially at night - would have a very demoralising effect on men in trenches, but there is little to fear for the flames attack only lasts 2 or 3 minutes. The flames are followed by dense clouds of black smoke.	
"	15"	9.A.M	Weather showery + cold. The M.G. Sgt went in a Bridge Head Scheme as a separate unit. Given task of carrying out action behind the enemy's entrenchments against movement points in the front. Many incidents for mostly afterwards return to permanent billets at CAUMONT - distance 15 miles.	

Army Form C. 2118.

2/1

WAR DIARY
or
INTELLIGENCE SUMMARY
(Erase heading not required.)

Instructions regarding War Diaries and Intelligence Summaries are contained in F. S. Regs., Part II. and the Staff Manual respectively. Title Pages will be prepared in manuscript.

Place	Date	Hour	Summary of Events and Information	Remarks and references to Appendices
CAUMONT.	16" 17" 18"	—	Weather very wet — heavy rain. All horses out in open owing to disinfection of stables against glanders. Mange not being passed by the Vet. Officer. See G.O.C. re question of reinforcements for British Regiments.	
	19" – 23" 24		Very wet weather, which prevented much work being done. Weather very fine. Tactical Exercise for C.O.'s under B.G.M. taken C.O.'s in the neighbourhood of ARGENVILLERS & YVRENEUEUX. The following points were brought out on the various exercises :— (a) Special Reconnaissances by Officer patrols. These were divided under two headings :— (i) Those sent out by the A.G. Commander to find out information about the enemy for the special purpose of mostly the A.G. These would be detailed by the A.G. Commander from the Main Guard. (ii) Those sent out by the G.O.C. on special missions. Such as to report to the enemy's use of roads – bridges – hostile dispositions to a distant area etc., & they will be detailed from the Main Body. (b) The necessity when detailing any patrol to give the Commander a definite mission, to clear instructions as to what is wanted (what his report should contain) – that he should be given a free hand to obtain the information asked for.	

Army Form C. 2118.

WAR DIARY
or
INTELLIGENCE SUMMARY
(Erase heading not required.)

Place	Date	Hour	Summary of Events and Information	Remarks and references to Appendices
[Aldershot]	16?		(Cont'd)(c) The duties of an O.C. Vanguard when first sent out — namely, to push out as far as possible the streams of dispatches of reconnaissance & no resistance to him — i.e. reconnaissance & not resistance. (d) The importance of not moving in masses — in no regular formation. (e) Communication between Brigades — is necessary for a officer to be sent by each G.O.C. to the other Brigades with orders. (f) The variety of ways of attacking a village with a body namely, of 1 Regt (Bn.) — 1 Group M. Guns & 1 Section R.H.A. (i) The plan decided on must depend on the shape & size of the village, the period on cover, flanks, — for instance, a long village running on period particularly to your front should be attacked from the end — not so from the flanks. (ii) Special & very definite instructions must be given to the C.O. Action R.H.A. — that mostly deferring the Target, to the time at which he is to left "his fire for it to a further object. (iii) to special task must also be allotted to the O.C. M.G. Troops — giving him the times at which he is to cease fire so as not to interfere with the attacking Troops. (g) That when an Advanced Guard, Square attacks a village, it divides as necessary becomes a Regimental Operation	

Army Form C. 2118.

WAR DIARY
INTELLIGENCE SUMMARY
(Erase heading not required.)

Instructions regarding War Diaries and Intelligence Summaries are contained in F. S. Regs., Part II. and the Staff Manual respectively. Title Pages will be prepared in manuscript.

Place	Date	Hour	Summary of Events and Information	Remarks and references to Appendices
CAUMONT	25-30	—	Weather very fine & warm. Fire coats held annual on range shortly - all 12 guns shooting exceptionally good.	

Lt. Carpenter Capt.
Cecil Latham M.G. Sqt.

SERIAL NO. 316.

Confidential

War Diary

of

Machine Gun Squadron, Canadian Corps Cavalry Brigade.

FROM 1st May 1916 TO 31st May 1916.

Army Form C. 2118.

WAR DIARY
of
INTELLIGENCE SUMMARY

(Erase heading not required.) LUCKNOW M.G. SQUADRON.

Instructions regarding War Diaries and Intelligence Summaries are contained in F. S. Regs., Part II. and the Staff Manual respectively. Title Pages will be prepared in manuscript.

Place	Date	Hour	Summary of Events and Information	Remarks and references to Appendices
CAUMONT	May 1st	9 AM	The M.G. Squadron marched with the Brigade for a nights training near ST RIQUIER. It goes into temporary billets in the small village of LE FESTEL.— Close to the area allotted for training.	
	2nd	7 AM	Divisional Field Day — exceptionally heavy hailstorm. Rendezvous at X roads close to village of BUSSUS-BUSSUEL. Very long wait before any movement took place. — then went forward but did nothing in particular the whole day.	
	3rd	7 AM	Divisional Field Day. Weather somewhat like yesterdays. Rendezvous at X roads between ARGENVILLERS & GAPENNES. Went here for 4 hours before any movement took place, then went to position of readiness, whence into the days work. Learnt 3 lessons (1) That no hurry or this day did not make use of their mobility. (2) That unnecessary delay was caused in the receipt & issuing of orders (3) That on receipt of orders it is necessary to give yourself time to the A.G. Commdr. so that the A.G. may wait some time to gather its position; The A.G. should be formed up in readiness to move & all no orders of O.C. A.G. so that on receipt A.G. should remain were at o.c.i moves to. further delay after the A.G. is in movement to further delay. After the A.G. is in movement the written orders for the Brigade Battery should be made out.	

WAR DIARY or INTELLIGENCE SUMMARY

Place	Date	Hour	Summary of Events and Information	Remarks and references to Appendices
LE FESTEL	4	7 A.M.	Divisional Field Day for Inspection by Lt.Genl. Hubert Gough, Commdg. Reserve Corps. Teams fire Rendez-vous at MAIZICOURT then moved to position of readiness at A.1.c.1 (S.water) behind TELLENCOURT WOOD on one side of the position. Genl. Gough after severely criticising the operation made the following remarks :- (1) Officers should take soldiering seriously, trust is not their profession, & Nothing lay down now yet. They should always be keen & alert, & always looking about them to see what they should do next. They should learn to economise men, & gave this confidence which cannot be done if mistakes are always being made. Their hands should always be busy being & moving & never allowed to rest. They should learn how to make use of the ground & to use cover. The turning of their men. (2) Mobility. Many Officers are too slow & do not make use of the fine power of mobility which the Cavalry should expect of the Horse gunners. They are too slow aged to movement to attack a position on foot which could be much more easily & quickly taken if the power of the mounted attack were known, by a mounted attack assisted by Artillery fire on the hostile lines. Dismounted attacks therefore showed never be resorted to by Cavalry to open fighting.	

Army Form C. 2118.

Instructions regarding War Diaries and Intelligence Summaries are contained in F. S. Regs., Part II. and the Staff Manual respectively. Title Pages will be prepared in manuscript.

WAR DIARY
or
INTELLIGENCE SUMMARY

(Erase heading not required.)

Place	Date	Hour	Summary of Events and Information	Remarks and references to Appendices
LE FESTEL	4"	7 AM	(3) In making flanking movements up is essential for the commander to make ample provision for the protection of his outer & most vulnerable flank. This should be done by a faintly strong body, such as M. Guns or even the spare attached to it. (4) Artillery. The artillery showed be deployed at the earliest opportunity in the fight so that to deploy towards of shells should be poured on hostile targets as early as possible — the artillery officers must deploy the greatest energy & keep up a continual fire from the very start.	
	5"	10 AM	Tactical Exercise under 13" Gard FASHION, pointing out in detail the mistakes made the previous day.	
	6"	9.30 AM	Divisional Exercise with 2"d in command assembly Brigades & Regiments as regards the tactical handling of M.Guns the following points were noticed: — (1) When M.Guns are attached to Reg"ts or Squadrons. The O.C.'s in most instances entirely disregard them, give them no orders, forget to detail an escort for them, & use them in a manner absolutely opposed to all the principles laid down for the tactical handling of M.Guns in action. (2) The fact of splitting up a M.G. Squadron & distributing sections to Reg"ts previously necessitates the loss of track of them for power of takes away from the hands of the Brigadier the reserve of fire that should remain in his hands to meet pre unforeseen emergencies	

Army Form C. 2118.

27

Instructions regarding War Diaries and Intelligence Summaries are contained in F.S. Regs., Part II. and the Staff Manual respectively. Title Pages will be prepared in manuscript.

WAR DIARY or INTELLIGENCE SUMMARY
(Erase heading not required.)

Place	Date	Hour	Summary of Events and Information	Remarks and references to Appendices
LE FESTEL	6.	—	(3) By splitting up the Squadron, & taking the M.G. Sgt. Commander without a command & the fig. Officer Cmdr. Transport to N.Z. to find no. of the Squadron were little more or two bodies.	
CAUMONT	7.	1.30 P.M	Return to permanent billets in CAUMONT arriving 4.30 P.M	
	8.	—	Weather - showery + cold.	
	9.	—	Very wet day.	
	10.	—	Move to new billeting area via QUOEUX - HARAVESNES - ROUGEFAY - VACQUERIE-le-Boucq - LIGNY FREVENT to MONVAL. Bde starting point CABANE Squadron parades 7.45 A.M. A & B Echelons at 8.A.M. Mobile Vet. Section & 80 Infantry also billeted in same village. Bde billeted as under :— { Bde M.Q. - "U"- Battery R.H.A. Jodhpur Lrs at REBREUVE. K. Dgs. at SIBIVILLE - SERIAOURT 29th L. at CONETTEMONT 36 J.M. at MONCHEAUX.	
	11.		Weather fine	
	12. }		Weather very wet	
	13.		Bt. General gone takes over command of the Lucknow Car. Bde.	
	14.		Fine. Visit by G.O.C. Lucknow Cav. Bde.	
	15.		Very heavy rain	

2449 Wt. W14957/M90 750,000 1/16 J.B.C. & A. Form/C.2118/12.

WAR DIARY or INTELLIGENCE SUMMARY

Army Form C. 2118.

Place	Date	Hour	Summary of Events and Information	Remarks and references to Appendices
HONVAL	MAY 16th 17th 18th		Weather fine	
		9.30 AM	Tactical Exercise of NCOs under Brigade Major D.S.O. at which he brought out the necessity of moving by bounds — the need for study by COs p[l]t. [leader] of the Tactical handling of Machine & Hotchkiss guns — & the absolute necessity of Group specific instruction to all subordinate Comdrs, whether in charge of a Sgt., Troop, or patrol.	
		3 PM	Inspection by G.O.C. of the horses of the M.G. Squadron. Though he highly commended the fitness & condition of the horses of No 29. & 30th Sections, he expressed his views strongly as to the condition & stable management of the horses of the R.S.D. Sections.	
	19th	9.30 AM	Tactical Exercise of 36 T.M.G. groups under G.O.C., at which he expressed himself satisfied at the tactical handling of the M.G. Sections concerned. He brought out the necessity when choosing M.G. positions to avoid prominent objects such as hedges, roads, houses, troops & stones etc, but important to make use of dips & fire phenom[ena] when the position can be approached unseen. He also pointed out the advantage in having all M. guns in position for the enemy's frontal etc. to keep most appeals how the No 3rd will never think of give away a M.G. position, if not located after by the Section Commander. Dismounted Capepts put on 4 hours machine [work].	
	20th		Tactical Exercise of 36th T.M. under G.O.C. The following points were brought out:	

29

Army Form C. 2118.

WAR DIARY
or
INTELLIGENCE SUMMARY
(Erase heading not required.)

Instructions regarding War Diaries and Intelligence Summaries are contained in F. S. Regs., Part II. and the Staff Manual respectively. Title Pages will be prepared in manuscript.

Place	Date	Hour	Summary of Events and Information	Remarks and references to Appendices
HONVAL	20		(Cont'd). (A) The necessity for a very careful personal reconnaissance when time admits "Time spent in reconnaissance is never wasted". (b) To keeping up a defensive position, in a favourable spot or position or trenches, which may be able to get close or to take the troops in their samples in position unprepared & to keep close behind. (c) If troops start shaping themselves on what they can be observed by the enemy, they will at once be fired on. These installation machine guns might be able to get into position unsuspected. (d) Whether or a little or dig in to the open or to occupy C copse, what units in all likelihood to shelter. Weather - very fine throughout.	
"	21 ⎫ 22 ⎬ 23 ⎭		Showers.	
"	24		Heavy rain. Inspection of the Squadron by the G. in C.	
"	25		General Sir Douglas Haig. Sanction received for an increase to the Establishment of a M.G. Squadron vide C.G.S. as under :- 1 Saddler, 1 Indian Clerk, 1 Asst. Surgeon, 1 Jemadar No. 0. B/936.7 G.H.Q. memo + 1 puckly for Sestrin, 1 farr Lance Serj', per Squadron, 2 privt Lance Corporal 14th May '16 per Lance Dafadars per Section.	No A.4363 of 21/5/16

*

WAR DIARY / INTELLIGENCE SUMMARY

Army Form C. 2118.

Place: HONVAL

Date	Hour	Summary of Events and Information	Remarks
25		In the "Defence of a Village" scheme, the advantage was brought out in installing the present with a few patrols and in heavy Machine & Hotchkiss guns in position so as to cover the present unit for. This arrangement allowed the main body of troops to rest.	
26		In a Tactical scheme set for 27 & 36/19 Guns. The following points were brought out (a) the great importance of watching all villages with M. Guns. Unsuitability of win rifles. (b) the necessity for each section having a range taken (c) the need for each section having a suitable. Attached on belonging to it so as to be able to communicate with other sections when in action. This is most important now that Telephones (field) have been issued to the Squadrons.	
27		Test March. This was practical to see that all arrangements for the sudden turnout of troops was correct, that the proper numbers of men, horses, vehicles were present & made arrived at the rendez-vous at the scheduled time.	
28 29 30 31		Divisional Scheme. No important points were noted.	

Lieut Colonel Staff Corps

June 1916 — 12 Squadron — Lucknow Bde.

WAR DIARY or ~~INTELLIGENCE SUMMARY~~

(Erase heading not required.)

Instructions regarding War Diaries and Intelligence Summaries are contained in F. S. Regs., Part II. and the Staff Manual respectively. Title Pages will be prepared in manuscript.

Army Form C. 2118.

207

Place	Date	Hour	Summary of Events and Information	Remarks and references to Appendices
HINVAL	June 1st	-	Weather - fine	
	2nd	-	G.O.C.'s Scheme for Jodhpore Lancers. The following points were brought out. -	
			(a) the advantage of personal reconnaissance for ground that may appear from a distance quite impossible & unsuitable for moving over may on being personally reconnoitred be found perfectly practicable for the massing & deployment of troops.	
			(b) the possibility of O.C. forgetting or not using to the best advantage sections of artillery under their orders.	
			(c) the necessity of considering in taking up a position whether it is likely to be shelled by the hostile guns	
			(d) the difficulties that arise in attacking & securing woods.	
	3rd		G.O.C.'s scheme for Hd Qrs. M Guns. On this occasion one gun was sent with the Advanced Guard & the other kept with the Main Body - thereby splitting up the command of the O.C. M.G. Section. This practice is very often adopted when sections are attached to Regiments - owing chiefly to the ignorance of some Regimental officers in the handling of M Guns.	
	5th		Inspection by the O.C. A.S.C. of all Transport in charge of the M.G. Squadron. Attention was drawn to necessity for careful overhaul of [illegible] fittings &c.	

32

Instructions regarding War Diaries and Intelligence Summaries are contained in F. S. Regs., Part II. and the Staff Manual respectively. Title Pages will be prepared in manuscript.

WAR DIARY
or
~~INTELLIGENCE SUMMARY~~

(Erase heading not required.)

Army Form C. 2118.

208

Place	Date	Hour	Summary of Events and Information	Remarks and references to Appendices
			and adjustment of harness, & the need for spare draught horses to replace those in Transport going lame etc. At present, the exact number of Transport horses as are necessary for the G.S. Wagon – 6 double limbered wagons & 2 water carts are kept up. No provision has been made in the event of any of the above horses going lame or sick. I am of opinion that at least two horses over & above what are actually required for the Transport should be permanently kept on charge to replace casualties.	
Havre	8.		The fact that many C.O.s dont as yet fully appreciate the value of M Guns & the necessity to assist their M.Gun [illegible] with good men & horses from their Regts. has again been brought up. They also dont seem to realize the importance of having always fully trained a 1st & 2nd Reserve for their M.G. Sections.	
	9.		Weather wet & cold.	
	10.		do do A trial was given to a patent arrangement sent to the Squadron to report on. It consisted of a metal case which could be fixed on the front cover of the Gun, in such a way as to allow the Gun to be brought into action fully loaded. The case contained a mech.[?] strips of 25 Cartridges & was found to be most satisfactory. The metal strips, also used for this[?], was ~~[illegible]~~ condemned owing to the rounds frequently jumping out of their clips when the gun was in action	

INTELLIGENCE SUMMARY

(Erase heading not required.)

Summary of Events and Information

Place	Date	Hour	Summary of Events and Information	Remarks and references to Appendices
HEBUTERNE	11		The question of the appointment of an M.G. Subaltern E. in Command of M.G. Subaltern, who should then not be If an extra Subaltern to M.G. Sections in the showing for M.G. Subaltern not a base for an extra M.G. Section — the Battalion would be insisted on if the two Ypres salients for the emergency Section should be some for the emergency Ind[en]ts should be encouraged. The short replacement of our gunnery will, it appears not to be replaced by the the Battalions has actually occurred — If the Co. in a Battn. M.G. Sgt has a certainty of his place is in our field by the Sgt's known a certainty this place in the field by the 2nd in Command who has not plenty to supervise is to & the handling the M.G. etc without on the Lewis guns — if he is to is not to return in place has to be taken by a Section Cmdr. into probably has never before had to handle any guns into his section. There is a serious fault in the present organisation to our men should be put upon Appendices. Many guns a week.	
	16		In the new aerial distribution to M.G. Sections An aerial T Square has provided for 6 lost after Evacuation & Station known now is been a step for the ordinary machine stations in this Squadron. dein communications in the known Inst apparently have new been convinced in this Squadron for these twenty four hours.	

SERIAL NO. 316.

Confidential
War Diary
of

Machine Gun Squadron Lucknow Cavalry Brigade.

FROM 1st July 1916 TO 31st July 1916.

34

Army Form C. 2118.

WAR DIARY
of 1st NEW M.G. SQUADRON
INTELLIGENCE SUMMARY

(Erase heading not required.)

Place	Date	Hour	Summary of Events and Information	Remarks and references to Appendices
LA FOLIE FARM near LUCHEUX	JULY 1st	7.30 AM	Assault by 3rd & 4th Armies launched at 7.30 A.M. in conjunction with French on the line MARICOURT - FRICOURT - LA BOISSELLE - THIEPVAL - BEAUMONT MAMEL - GOMMECOURT. Villages of MARICOURT - MONTAUBAN - MAMETZ & LA BOISSELLE were captured. 1500 prisoners were taken, & 3000 by the French attacking on our Right & S. of River SOMME.	
FROHEN-le-PETIT.	2nd	6 P.M.	Move at short notice to FROHEN - le - PETIT via LUCHEUX - AROUCHES - HOUSSÉE - RANSART - BARLY - REMAISNIL. Lucknow Brigade billeted as follows:- At FROHEN - le - Grand & le Petit — B.H.Q. - K.D.G. M.G.S. & M.V.S — 29th L. & 36 J.H. At VILLERS - L'Hôpital. This sudden & unexpected order to move brought out the necessity of having every thing absolutely ready for an immediate move — it is to have saddles properly fitted with marching order & places in front of their horses, to have limbers & G.S. Wagons as far as possible correctly loaded. A large quantity of unnecessary & useless stuff was put in the Wagons at the last moment, which showed the need for more frequent & careful inspections of the men's kits. All kits carefully inspected & reloaded on wagons as per Schedule. The Shortage of Transport for a M.G. Squadron	
"	3rd			

WAR DIARY / INTELLIGENCE SUMMARY

Army Form C. 2118.

Place	Date	Hour	Summary of Events and Information	Remarks and references to Appendices
FROHEN-le-PETIT	4=		Practice taking guns, ammunition, & personnel across the River AUTHIE in action divisions. To take the leader of its wheels to pull it backwards upwards across the river was found to be the best & fastest means of getting the section across as was necessary however, to have the opening in the hedges previously filled up with tree-branches, so as to stop the wheels getting in. The following impressions/points were noted — (1) To save time a reconnoissance should be carefully worked out & gone through on the work is assaulted. (2) Drag-ropes & other details must be carefully inspected beforehand. (3) Every man must be properly cast off & carefully explained his duties beforehand.	
	5=		When the K.O.Y. section was practicing crossing enemy the river — Pte Curran got cramp in mid-stream & had it not been for the prompt action of Private MACHELL in diving in to this rescue — Pte Curran would undoubtedly have been drowned.	

WAR DIARY or INTELLIGENCE SUMMARY

Army Form C. 2118.

Place: FRONON / L. Palot

Date	Hour	Summary of Events and Information	Remarks and references to Appendices
7:		Heavy rain. Watch a specimen of the K.A.S's dressing the horses in 3 different ways:— (a) G.S. wagon inspected. Tarpaulin stuffed with straw — very good — fair. (b) 1/2 limber wagon ". The Tarpaulin or straw was not really necessary. (c) K.G.F. made of wagon sheets stuffed with straw — but a tremendous trouble to tie up, 6 lances too long to tie — a good arrangement for use but etc. suggested make, & the straw tremendous etc. suggested. Inspection rifle when wounded.	
8:		G.O.C.'s inspection of 29. b. section (under L.P. Paterson). Crossing the river by means of 7 & half burthen for saddles & coiled telephone wire for guns harnesses & Harness. Time taken for whole section — 40 mins. The telephone boil borrowed & 11 strands whose wire found sufficient to take the guns ammunition & personnel across. (vide sketch inside)	

WAR DIARY
or
INTELLIGENCE SUMMARY
(Erase heading not required.)

Army Form C. 2118.

Place	Date	Hour	Summary of Events and Information	Remarks and references to Appendices
FROMEN-le-POPS	8th	11--	G.O.C's inspection of M.G. Squadron in Marching Order. The following points were brought out:—	

(A) The alteration of the EASSIE bundle under the saddle except for general cases of bad sore backs

(B) The necessity for more attention being paid by O.C Sections to detail (especially in the British Sections)

(C) The need for uniformity

(d) Daily inspection of all arms & ammunition (especially with regard to the armament of the Squadron & the British Seatings)

(E) The necessity for troops to carry the contents of one emergency ration.

[Sketch diagram showing: Telephone wire, Timber pole, Nails, Pegs/ropes, Stirrup iron, 11 Chains, M.guns & Tripods, Small-up appts, Reins, Cover, Tree]

Place	Date	Hour	Summary of Events and Information	Remarks and references to Appendices
FROMEL- LES	12.		A through inspection of points brought out at G.O.C's inspection on previous day.	
"	14.		Inspection of dismounted men, vehicles at results of gunnery training. As regards the Lewis Gun, it appears too much time has been spent on mechanism & not sufficient on stoppages, loading, mounting & dismounting gun etc.	
"	15.		Field Firing. Control of gun by telephone - quite satisfactory if telephone is placed at a distance of 20' from guns when firing. It took exactly 7 minutes to establish communication with all guns. I consider telephone communication is absolutely essential for the M.G. Squadron. If the guns are in action on a defensive position or at night, for it is not only ranges, cavalier, but prevents the pm positions being given away by noises too lightly normal orders to gun teams etc.	

Army Form C. 2118.

WAR DIARY
or
INTELLIGENCE SUMMARY
(Erase heading not required.)

Instructions regarding War Diaries and Intelligence Summaries are contained in F. S. Regs., Part II. and the Staff Manual respectively. Title Pages will be prepared in manuscript.

39

Place	Date	Hour	Summary of Events and Information	Remarks and references to Appendices
FROHEN-le-Petit	18		Three of the Telephones & Exchange in charge of the Squadron as taken away by order of the Division & transferred to O.C. Brigade Signals. This has during with all the practice the Squadron has been months in controlling fire by phone, & I consider will greatly affect the efficiency of the guns when in action, no states in previous page.	
BETHONCOURT	19		Move to new area near AUBIGNY. March 7½ at 9 A.M. 9 remat billets at BETHENCOURT by 4.40 P.M./ distance 20 miles./ moving by VILLERS-L'hôpital – BONNIERES-REBREUVIETTE – AMEINES & SAVY. 18th Cheshire labour Battn also billeted in this village. Practice indences & night firing with all sections.	
"	21			
	22		The new transing & telegating drill are found to be most satisfactory provided they are never adjusted with care, but the accuracy of	

Army Form C. 2118.

WAR DIARY
or
INTELLIGENCE SUMMARY
(Erase heading not required.)

Place	Date	Hour	Summary of Events and Information	Remarks and references to Appendices
BETHENCOURT	25		The maps were clearly brought out the necessity for checking the drawings to every target. Schemes under G.O.C. attack on enemy Points noted :— (a) Proper standing round the gun. (b) Necessity to see bottom edge of target when firing. (c) Proper arrangements for communication with all guns. (d) Advantages of cross fire.	
	26 27		Field firing all sections. The shooting was excellent especially on Lewis sections. The order were good, but the difficulties that were made to the Brit Officer is knowing our own very clearly illustrated.	
	31		Tactical Ride made G.O.C.	

M.L. Carpenter Capt
Cmdt [?] M.G Squadron

SERIAL NO. 316.

Confidential
War Diary
of

Machine Gun Squadron, Lucknow Cavalry Brigade.

FROM 1st August 1916 TO 31st August 1916.

Army Form C. 2118.

WAR DIARY
OF
INTELLIGENCE SUMMARY

(Erase heading not required.)

Instructions regarding War Diaries and Intelligence Summaries are contained in F.S. Regs., Part II. and the Staff Manual respectively. Title Pages will be prepared in manuscript.

Place	Date	Hour	Summary of Events and Information	Remarks and references to Appendices
BETHENCOURT	August 1st		No change	
	2nd		"	
	3rd		Interpreter VIEILLOT transferred from M.G. Sqd. & ordered to report himself to 3rd Army H.Q. St Pol.	
	4th		No change	
	5th		"	
	6th		All Divisions have attached to sections upon their own Units temporarily.	
	7th		The two H.Dq. M.G. Sections are detailed for special duty & move to BRYAS - 2½ mil. N.E. of ST POL.	
	8th	9 A.M.	Bin Brigade moves into VII Corps area, and is attached for work to 46th & 56th Divisions.	
HUMBERCOURT	9th	8.45 AM	The M.G. Squadron (less 4 sections) moves to HUMBERCOURT Via MAIZIERES, SARS-LES-BOIS - LIENCOURT - GRAND RULLECOURT & WARLUZEL. (Pte LENS map No 11.)	
			Interpreter R QUANTIN joins the Squadron Via Infanterie VIEILLOT Reinforced.	
	10th		No change	
	11th		"	
	12th		2nd A & F WOOD att'd 36th Infantry Bde. Capt. LANCASTER & L/Corpl DAVIES M.G. Corps proceed to M.G. School	
	13th		at CASSIERS for an Advanced Course of Training.	
	14th		4 reinforcements from M.G. Corps Base report their arrival & are taken on the strength of the Squadron.	
	15th		No change	
	16th		"	
	17th		Capt. J GRAVES evacuated sick. 2nd Lt OGLEY I A R att'd 36 J H taken over command of his Section.	
	18th		No change	
	19th		"	
	20th		31st HQ. M.G. Section changes places with 36th Section & attached to 36th North Heros	
	21st			

Army Form C. 2118.

WAR DIARY
INTELLIGENCE SUMMARY
(Erase heading not required.)

Place	Date	Hour	Summary of Events and Information	Remarks and references to Appendices
HUMBERCOURT	22		No change.	ay
	23		"	ay
	24		"	ay
	25		1 R.A.M.C. Orderly joined & is taken on strength of Squadron vice Pte HENTHORNE evacuated	ay
	26		No change	ay
	27		Lieut. HOWELL P.L.H. attached 35 Infantry Brigade taken over command of No 5 M.G. Section vice 2/Lt OGLEY returned to unit	ay
	28		No change	ay
	29		1 N.CO. + 8 men arrive from M.G.C. Base as reinforcements	ay
	30		No change	ay
	31			ay

John Carpenter Capt S

Comd^g Lucknow M.G. Squadron

SERIAL N0. 316.

Confidential
War Diary
of

Machine Gun Squadron, Lucknow Cavalry Brigade.

FROM 1st September 1916 TO 30th September 1916

Army Form C. 2118.

WAR DIARY
INTELLIGENCE SUMMARY

(Erase heading not required.)

Instructions regarding War Diaries and Intelligence Summaries are contained in F. S. Regs., Part II. and the Staff Manual respectively. Title Pages will be prepared in manuscript.

40

Place	Date	Hour	Summary of Events and Information	Remarks and references to Appendices
		1916.		
HUMBERCOURT	Sept 1st		No change	Inl
"	2nd		No change	Inl
OCCOCHES	3rd	9.30 AM	The M.G. Squadron (less 3 sections) marched to OCCOCHES via LUCHEUX. BOUQUEMAISON & NEUVILLETTE	Inl
BRAILLY	4th	10	" " " " " " FROHEN-le-grand - MAIZICOURT - ARGENVILLERS & BRAILLY	Inl
	5th		and NOYELLE-en-CHAUSSÉE. (vide ABBEVILLE map. No. 14. 1/100,000)	Inl
"	6th		Went on St RIQUIER Training area.	Inl
"	7th		" " " "	Inl
"	8th		" " " "	Inl
"	9th		" " " "	Inl
"	10th		" " " "	Inl
FROHEN-le-Petit	11		M.G.Sq (less 3 sections) marched to FROHEN-le-Petit via NOYELLE-en-CHAUSSÉE - NEUILLY-le-Dien - ACQUET - AUXI-le-CHATEAU.	Inl
GROUCHES	12		" " " GROUCHES via HEM - HAUTE VISÉE (south) LENS map.	Inl
			Took over command from Capt. G. A. Crawford "No Car App"	Gun
QUERRIEUX	13		" " " QUERRIEUX via BEAUVAL, TALMAS. " "	Rain
	14		" " " to AIRIEME near QUERRIEUX -	Rain
DERNANCOURT	15		" " " marched to bivouac near DERNANCOURT at 5 am (near "B" echelon)	Rain
"	16		No change. 1 horse, 36 section wounded	Rain
"	17		No change - Capt. G. A. Mercer & Lieut Holt made reconnaissance of town up to LONGUEVAL	Rain
"	18		No change - Eight horses arrive from remount depot + two wagons	Rain

Army Form C. 2118.

WAR DIARY
or
INTELLIGENCE SUMMARY

(Erase heading not required.)

Place	Date	Hour	Summary of Events and Information	Remarks and references to Appendices
DERNANCOURT	Sept. 19-	9.30 am	No change —	aam.
"	20-	10 am	Capt. Aherne + Lieut Wark reconnoitred cavalry track to LONGUEVAL —	aam.
"	21st	"	M.G. Squadron has 3 sections still in bivouac — Farrier Serg.t Bailey arrived from base —	aam.
"	22nd	"	No change — " —	aam.
"	23rd	"	No change —	aam.
"	24th	"	Lieut Hassall reconnoitred Track to FLERS. Lieut Falconer sent to position of reserve transport camp self — Rod'e over the road to them at an hour later — Capt. Aherne attended conference of C.O.'s at B.H.Q — situation explained — Lieut O'Connor joined Squadron from M.G. School + Took on command of No 3 Section —	aam.
"	25th		No change —	aam.
"	26th		Received order to saddle up 1.45 p.m. stood to saddle until 4.30. when order received to move to MAMETZ. The squadron arrived at MAMETZ at 7.30 p.m. and went into bivouac — Capt Hearne went forward with C.O.s to ascertain report centre at MONTAUBAN about 3 p.m. Headquarters of MAMETZ brigade at 11.30 p.m.	aam.

Army Form C. 2118.

WAR DIARY or INTELLIGENCE SUMMARY

(Erase heading not required.)

Place	Date	Hour	Summary of Events and Information	Remarks and references to Appendices
MAMETZ BUSSY-lès-DOURS	27	—	The M.G. Squadron received orders to march at 9 a.m. to old bivouac near DERNACOURT. Then a halt of 4 hours for watering & feeding. Marched again in rear of Brigade to bivouac near BUSSY-LES-DOURS arriving there at 7.15 p.m.	Rain.
		8.30 p.m.		
HANGEST	28	8.30 p.m.	The M.G. Squadron marched at 8.30 a.m. to close billets at HANGEST. Watering party under Lieut. Truell with interpreter sent on at 7 a.m. route via AMIENS – PICQUIGNY. Arrived at billets at 3.15, having been cut off by traffic near AMIENS.	Rain.
EAUCOURT Sur-Somme	29	9 p.m.	The M.G. Squadron marched with the Brigade at 8.30 a.m. to close billets in EAUCOURT-S-SOMME via CONDÉ-FOLIE – L'ETOILE – PONT-REMY –	Rain.
CRECY	30	10 p.m.	The Brigade marched at 8.30 a.m. from starting point north of A in ABBEVILLE to close billets in CRECY area. The M.G. Squadron arrived at its billets at 1.30 p.m. Some of the horses showed signs of fatigue but on the whole the horses of the Squadron have stood the marches very well.	Rain.

A.A. Murray
Capt.
Comdg. Machine Gun Squadron

SERIAL NO. 316.

Confidential
War Diary
of

Machine Gun Squadron, Lucknow Cavalry Brigade.

FROM 1st October 1916 TO 31st October 1915.
30th November 1916

WAR DIARY
or
INTELLIGENCE SUMMARY
(Erase heading not required.)

Army Form C. 2118.

M.G. Sqdn. Lucknow Bde.

Place	Date	Hour	Summary of Events and Information	Remarks and references to Appendices
CRECY	Oct. 1	8 p.m.	The Squadron remained in Billets.	Rain.
"	2nd	8 p.m.	No change - Sr. Nain Singh 2gt. Sick - evacuated to Hospital.	Rain.
"	3rd	8 p.m.	No change.	Rain.
"	4th	8 p.m.	No change - Pte. Jenkins M.G.C No. 2 Section - Sick - evacuated to Hospital. Pte. Bryard M.G.C. reported this morning from leave.	Rain.
"	5	8 p.m.	No change.	Rain.
"	6	8 p.m.	No change. Sr. Mohan Singh 22nd Cav. y. joined the Squadron as Clerk.	Rain.
BUIGNY	7	8 p.m.	The M.G. Squadron (all sections) marched to BUIGNY. for field firing practice. Arrived there at 6 p.m.	Rain.
CRECY	8	6 p.m.	After field firing practice the M.G. Squadron marched back to billets at CRECY. leaving BUIGNY at 2.30 p.m. route through FORET de CRECY. Pte. Buchan M.G.C. evacuated sick to Hospital.	Rain.
"	9	8 p.m.	The Squadron took part in Divisional Scheme under Corps Commander. No change.	Rain.
"	10		No change.	Rain.
"	11	8 p.m.	No change.	Rain.

Army Form C. 2118.

WAR DIARY
or
INTELLIGENCE SUMMARY
(Erase heading not required.)

Instructions regarding War Diaries and Intelligence Summaries are contained in F. S. Regs., Part II. and the Staff Manual respectively. Title Pages will be prepared in manuscript.

Place	Date	Hour	Summary of Events and Information	Remarks and references to Appendices
CRECY	12	8 p.m.	No changes. Lt Howell admitted to hospital – 8 Remounts arrived from Remount Depot –	Rain
"	13	8 p.m.	No change – No 5 Section transferred to Regt for one month – No. 6, Nigerian Squadron – Lt. Sher Khan reported arrived from Base –	Rain
"	14	8 p.m.	No changes – No. 4 & 2 Sections from Thani Regts and No 1 and 3 from Nigerian Squadron –	Rain
"	15	8 p.m.	No change –	Rain
"	16	8 p.m.	No change, 6 horses evacuated through Mobile Vet Sectn.	Rain
"	17	8 p.m.	No change.	Rain
"	18	8 p.m.	No change.	Rain
"	19	8 p.m.	Recd. orders to h. horses & men to Winches on 21st. horses to h. handed over to Regts.	Rain
"	20	8 p.m.	All horses handed in to Regts except advance transport – spare kit dumped under care of Gendarmerie at CRECY – 205 of all ranks 10/9 off for French party.	Rain
"	21	8 p.m.	Remain'r limho until train was left at 8 a.m. for OCCHES.	Rain

2449 Wt. W14957/M90 750,000 1/16 J.B.C. & A. Forms/C.2118/12.

Army Form C. 2118.

WAR DIARY
or
INTELLIGENCE SUMMARY.
(Erase heading not required.)

Place	Date	Hour	Summary of Events and Information	Remarks and references to Appendices
SAILLY au BOIS.	Oct 22ⁿᵈ	8 p.m.	178 of all ranks embussed at 8 a.m. at CRECY - The rest of the convoy with SIALKOT + MHOW Jowid at FONTAINE-SUR-MAYE and LEBROYE - Reached SAILLY at -	
		1 P.M.	arranged billets for men - Red orders from Major Martin allotting a sector i.e. HEBUTERNE from WARRIOR to CEMETERY Trenches for LUCKNOW BDE.	
			made personal reconnaissance with Lieuts Hill + Gardner and struck from 3 p.m.	
		7.30	arranged gun positions - Reported to Brigade H.Q. (93ʳᵈ) at 10.30 p.m.	
			road HEBUTERNE to SAILLY Shelled with tear + gas shells.	O.a.h.
HEBUTERNE	23ʳᵈ	8 p.m.	Nos. 1, 2, + 4 Sections with six men per gun in position by 5 p.m. - Nos. 3, 5 and 6 sections arrived at 7.30 p.m. Kit unloaded and limbers Sub-took to COIGNEUX under S.Q.M.S. Addison - Enemy put barrage of 9 ns + Tear shells between HEBUTERNE + SAILLY between 5 p.m. + 8.30 p.m. Dug-outs arranged for all men of 1, 2, + 4 sections, and temporary accommodation for sections 3, 5 + 6. - H.Qrs. L.M.G.S. in GENEVIEVE Trench.	R.a.m.
do	24ᵗʰ		Personally reconnoitred entire sector again and placed Nos. 3, 5, + 6 Section improved positions + cleared up dug outs. All day post poned.	O.a.m.

WAR DIARY or INTELLIGENCE SUMMARY

Army Form C. 2118.

Place	Date	Hour	Summary of Events and Information	Remarks and references to Appendices
HEBUTERNE	25th	8 pm	HEBUTERNE vicinity shelled during night with gas shells both LT ward + HT during all target ranges, angles of elevation, usual angles completed to each gun - all available men put to improving dugouts and making alternative emplacements - a large no. of HE + S.A. shells over battery occupied by No. 1,2+4 sections during afternoon	R.A.W.
do.	26th	8 pm	Attack postponed - during the night our gas was discharged from front line - enemy retaliated with gas shells. No. 2 section position. New emplacements were built. to be completed at night.	
do.	27th	8 pm	HEBUTERNE shewing shelled also gun positions in PASTEUR, BOYER, BATTERSEA and BALLOON. No. 4 sections alternative emplacements begun a.m. New one commenced - Lt Howell took sub - military exit during afternoon.	Rain
do.	28th	8 pm	observation hut - all guns crews relieved from teams ? at SAILLY -	
No.1/4 Capt Simionds assumed Command M.G. Squadron at CRECY			to privately heavy on PASTEUR position - Lt Howell evacuated to hospital suffering from slight gas poisoning -	R.A.W.
do.	29	8 pm.	No.1 section pro tem shelled Hlom. en - No.3+4 section fired on large enemy fatigue during the night.	R.A.W.

WAR DIARY or INTELLIGENCE SUMMARY

Army Form C. 2118.

Place	Date	Hour	Summary of Events and Information	Remarks and references to Appendices
	Oct			
HEBUTERNE	30th	8 p.m.	X day postponed - No 4 & 5 sections positions harrowed by enemy M.G.S. AEIBUTERNE shelled intermittently throughout the day. Reported at 93rd Bde H.Q.s. No 1 Sect + No 3. fired on enemy's wire during night - all guns were ranged by short bursts. observing officers to sift gr. enough in front line	Rain
	31st	3 p.m.	Intermittent shelling of our positions during the day. I went to COIGNEUX and found all transport in order - at SAILLY were comfortable and had lately arranged scrounges by K/C carried out a N.C.M.'s ½ day upon footwear. Arr'd 3 hrs per gun and one N.C.O. per section being kept in the trenches No. 4 & 5 sections firing would support during the night	Rain

31.10.16.

A. Athorey
Capt.
for O.C. 11th MGC Bde 1st

Army Form C. 2118.

Lucknow M.G. Sqdn

WAR DIARY
INTELLIGENCE SUMMARY.

(Erase heading not required.)

Instructions regarding War Diaries and Intelligence Summaries are contained in F. S. Regs., Part II, and the Staff Manual respectively. Title pages will be prepared in manuscript.

Hour, Date, Place.	Summary of Events and Information.	Remarks and references to Appendices.
HEBUTERNE November 1st 1916 8 p.m.	Owing to weather conditions working parties were necessary all day clearing out water from trenches and repairing emplacements. No. 1, 2, + 3. Sect's assisted infantry patrols both retired fire during the night - 2500 rounds were fired - Lieut MARCOCK SALTY for not and 6 company details - Enemy shelling normal except at Northern end of PALLISSIER when it was heavy from 2 p.m. - to 4 p.m.	aam.
" Nov. 2nd 8 p.m.	No. 1, 4, 5 + 6 Sections fired on laid targets during the night - enemy replied with machine gun fire and H.F. Shells intermittently during the night - Several direct hits on SOUTH and BATTHURST - GAS ALERT during night -	aam.
" Nov. 3rd 8 p.m.	X day again postponed - working parties busy all day clearing water out of dug outs, trenches repairing emplacements, and communicating new dug out - trenches and sand bags officers trenches. No. 1, 2, 3, + 6 Sections assisted infantry patrols by machine gun fire in laid targets during the night.	aam.

WAR DIARY
or
INTELLIGENCE SUMMARY.
(Erase heading not required.)

Army Form C. 2118.

Hour, Date, Place.	Summary of Events and Information.	Remarks and references to Appendices.
HEBUTERNE. Nov. 4th 8 p.m.	A quiet night - only No 3. Section in action. N/md Target - at 4.30 a.m. Enemy briskly bombarded area between HEBUTERNE and CEMETERY - a working party of 12 men told off to assist SIALKOT B.S. S&M in making a new dug out - 2/Lt Rahmad Khan 36TH - S. Khan Mahomed 36TH and S. Mahomed Beg Syl. severely wounded by HE while working with this party - two M.G's in action against enemy aeroplane at 4.30 p.m. the fire appeared effective. Condition of Trenches bad - hit French tanks having been followed downpour then first in bringing them.	Rain.
" Nov. 5th 8 p.m.	Sepoy GULAM KHAZA 36TH killed by shell at 7 a.m. while visiting sentries. No 2 & 3 Sections in action during night - Enemy briskly bombarded HEBURTERNE and Northern and Chaulnes Sector between 4.30 p.m. and 6 p.m. no real work done by detachments in drying and repairing trenches -	Rain.

Army Form C. 2118.

WAR DIARY
or
INTELLIGENCE SUMMARY.
(Erase heading not required.)

Instructions regarding War Diaries and Intelligence Summaries are contained in F. S. Regs., Part II, and the Staff Manual respectively. Title pages will be prepared in manuscript.

Hour, Date, Place.	Summary of Events and Information.	Remarks and references to Appendices.
HEBUTERNE. Nov. 6th 8 p.m.	G.O.C. Lucknow Brigade visited Sparham at 1 p.m. No. 1 & 3 Section guns fired on enemy & our forward positions and fired on enemy lines during the night. Enemy's shelling normal. Gas alert during the night – 1/D Rahmal Khan died of wounds at Casualty Clearing Station.	Rain
" Nov. 7th 8 p.m.	All Section guns co-operated with infantry during the night – covering trench raids – Artillery co-operated with intense bombardment of enemy lines – Enemy reply feeble, had a good many shells mostly gas fell in Northern half of Luckow Sector during 15 day. No 1 and 3 Section "guns in action against Enemy aeroplane at 3.20 p.m and 5 p.m Heavy rain & Trenches falling in badly especially SOMME.	RAIN.
" Nov. 8th 8 p.m.	No 5 & 6 Sections fired in enemy lines and assisted infantry patrols with machine gun during the night. Enemy machine gun fire – pretty continuous – shelling normal. No 2 section in action against enemy aeroplane at 1.07000 m, 2.55 p.m, and 4.30 p.m.	Rain.

Gulab Singh & Sons, Calcutta—No. 22 Army C.—5-8-14—1,07,000.

WAR DIARY or INTELLIGENCE SUMMARY

Army Form C. 2118.

(Erase heading not required.)

Hour, Date, Place.	Summary of Events and Information.	Remarks and references to Appendices.
HEBUTERNE Nov 8th 6 p.m.	Extra Helio troops up from SAILLY trench – some fatiguing had – 8ft deep with several dug outs started –	RAW
" Nov 9th 8 p.m.	Alternate guns from each section fired during the night – enemy shelling this Targets during the night – enemy shelling this normal – No 2 + 3 Sections in action opposite enemy trenches – Ch. avaiante men clearing up and cleaning out trenches –	RAW
" Nov 10th 8 p.m.	All Sections again relieved and Lieut HOLT sent to SAILLY trench to WARD – enemy Keep quiet in the air – during the afternoon – guns from No 1.2. 3. 4 + 6 Sections assisted in Holding their own infantry raid during the night – at 4.30 p.m. Lt. Col. HOLLIS Kt. Lot. 10th Mach. Coy. – 2 new emplacements replacing 2 guns in forward position intact. Completed and preliminary arrangements made shelling normal –	RAW

Army Form C. 2118.

WAR DIARY
or
INTELLIGENCE SUMMARY.
(Erase heading not required.)

Hour, Date, Place.	Summary of Events and Information.	Remarks and references to Appendices.
HEBUTERNE Nov 11th 1916. 8 p.m.	X. day - during the night SAILLY heavily shelled with gas shells - hermit bomb for four hours - Enemy gun very active and bombardment from WARRIOR SAP intermittent with H.E. and shrapnel - No.1 sect. Amm: dump hit by H.E. and several boxes of S.A.A. exploded. Operation took from 7.30 p.m. to 1.30 a.m. building emplacements for trench guns in saps - in front of KNOX trench all final arrangements for 2 day completed - and relief of trenches carried th[rough] up by 12.30 a.m. 12th Instant remainder of men mind touch COIGNEUX huts S.A.A.S. Additional two more current emplacements completed and reinforced. No 1 + 5 sectors assisting infantry during night with work allowed this in trench attacks intense lately to maintain task lists.	aar.

WAR DIARY
or
INTELLIGENCE SUMMARY.

Army Form C. 2118.

(Erase heading not required.)

Hour, Date, Place.	Summary of Events and Information.	Remarks and references to Appendices.
HEBUTERNE. Nov.12th 1916. 8 p.m.	Enemy fired a number of gas shells during the night at N-50 feet in CEMETERY - remainder directed at batteries between HEBUTERNE & SAILLY - New trench gun positions inspired and fresh arrangements made for Z. day. At 8.30 a.m. all attacks at SAILLY left for COIGNEUX and all ten trench & Trucks arrived under Lieut HOLT at 12 midday - found other trench mortar officer & Sergt to immediate and all positions inspected - 7.30 p.m. L/7 pioneers started at H8gr dugout that K.B.C. gun under Sergt Stratford had started to move forward position and at 7.00 to left with 13ge'L. gun & forward position - Y.day.	a.m.
" Nov.13th 1916 11.45 p.m.	At 5. a.m. rec'd reports from all Section commanders that all ready to open fire - watches having been synchronised at 11. p.m. 12th inst - At 5.45 a.m. all guns opened on laid targets - firing at the rate of 1000 rounds per hour. Very misty and observation bad -	

Army Form C. 2118.

WAR DIARY
or
INTELLIGENCE SUMMARY

(Erase heading not required.)

Instructions regarding War Diaries and Intelligence Summaries are contained in F. S. Regs., Part II. and the Staff Manual respectively. Title Pages will be prepared in manuscript.

Place	Date	Hour	Summary of Events and Information	Remarks and references to Appendices
HAUTERNE.	13th Nov 1916.	11.45 p.m.	At 7. a.m. rcd. all wire report from all section commanders — S.S.M. Webb, that put in command of No. 5 Section. This section being without an officer or senior N.C.O. Enemy officer — at 7.30 a.m. commenced shelling — but only intermittently, and chiefly H.E. on PALLISSER + SONIS — at 7.45 a.m. Lieut O'Connor reported that BATTEUSE and PALLISSER were being bombarded by M.G. from direction of SERRE road — at 4/4/12 SOWAR SINGH reported wounded by M.G. hit — at 8.20 a.m. Lieut Falconar reported enemy putting heavy barrage on KNOT — and virtually searching JEAN BART + JENA. St. RATTAN SINGH wounded — 10.30 a.m. Lieut WARD reports enemy shelling SONIS + NIGHTJON heavily — No 2. Section drgnt. Kerr in — Lieut O'Connor reports PALLISSER + SERRE ROAD being heavily shelled — Sr. KATAR SINGH killed — while returning with message — 10.45 a.m. Lieut FALCONAR reports shelling W'less in KNOT. Several men hit — at 11. a.m. Sect. 3 men as reinforcements to Lieut FALCONAR — Sr. KHAZAN SINGH, MAHOMED HAFIZ, SAPS DARRO SINGH, RYA DURHAM SINGH, St. SINGH RAM wounded — 11.30. a.m. at wire report — recd. from Lieut WARD. No report from forward guns — 12.30 p.m. rcd. report from Serg. Strathml. (in charge right forward gun) that Lieut FALCONAR wounded — and all the crew of left gun except A/D. Durham Singh laid nt — reinforcements at once sent. worry down — Commandig. ordered Lieut HOLT to relieve Lieut FALCONAR, at 1.20 p.m. recd. report signed by Lieut FALCONAR saying he would stay with gun until relieved — and asking for more men — at 12. noon shed reserved all guns + slacken fire to 500 rounds per hour — at 1.45 p.m. Lieut HOLT reported at H.Qs. August on his way down where Lieut FALCONAR, he left with him 2 more reinforcements and a guide from No. 2. Sect.	

2449 Wt. W14957/M90 750,000 1/16 J.B.C. & A. Forms/C.2118/12

Army Form C. 2118.

WAR DIARY
or
INTELLIGENCE SUMMARY
(Erase heading not required.)

Place	Date	Hour	Summary of Events and Information	Remarks and references to Appendices
REBUTERNE	13th NOV.	11.45 p.m.	At 2.20 p.m. rec'd 8th wire report from LIEUT WARD + LIEUT O'CONNOR — at 3.10 p.m. rec'd information from B.M. 93rd Bde that the enemy were massing for a counter attack opposite the POINT — and WEST OF STARR WOOD — CAPT WINSLER — O.C. BLINKER (combined M.G. Coys) ordered all guns tearing on K. Lev ground west of STARR WOOD and LADOUVIERE FARM by 3.20 p.m. all Luekins guns reported laid tearing at 1500 rounds per hour in new target — Pt 6188 did excellent work as arranged on this occasion reaching No. 1 + 2 Section positions in 5 minutes in the open — at 4.20 p.m. LIEUT FALCONAR arrived at M.G. dugout — he reported that he had not seen LIEUT HOLT, but that JEMDR THAN SINGH + 2 men had reached him in 3.20 p.m. he had been able to get an open target near the POINT — and with RED JURMAN SINGH a No. 2 of the gun — had been able to hit 4 M.G.'s at the enemy at range 500 yds to 600 yds — that were from 200 to 300 of them. They immediately went back to their trenches. Had him sent to dressing station at once — at 4.35 p.m. LIEUT HOLT arrived — having been waited that through the barrage at junction of JEAN BART — leaving — he had come back through BRISEAU — and when he reached The corner of JEAN BART had entire trench blown in and the infantry fast at the trench junction just leaving — as this left the forward guns w. the air. I opened at once to 93rd Bde — and rec'd an answer that the infantry was to hold this front and was to return at once — at 5.45 p.m. a complete relief having started from No. 1 + 2 Sections — under Sergt. Coffey. Both the forward guns w 'meantime Sergt Slicing had reported drawn to forward guns. LIEUT HOLT reported Ptes PORTER	

2449 Wt. W14957/M90 750,000 1/16 J.B.C. & A. Forms/C.2118/12.

Place	Date	Hour	Summary of Events and Information	Remarks and references to Appendices
HEBUTERNE	13th Nov.	11:45 pm	and BOLTON to casualties, and the gun out of action by enemy MG fire — So I took No gun from 36th No. 6 Section — and party of carriers which knew from 36th with relief party to forward position — at 5:35 I had also returned other relieving rescue hut to clear guns — remaining handy to open fire at once with LIEUTHOLT's party going out in the open — (No. hth. JEAN BART & JENA were improvements) Reached forward gun position without any casualties — relief was immediately arranged — and new gun mounted. Pte PORTER had his shell after being hit. Pte BOLTON and others to dressing station by 36th. Stretcher bearers after assuring myself that both guns were in order & crew fit. I returned to HQ. and sent return to Lieut O'CONNOR the prepared to relieve Lieut HOLT at 4 a.m. with which to hth. Sgt. PADGE guns — Several men casualties were reported accident & dressing station between 5:30 pm and 8:30 pm. At which reports rec'd from No. 12, 13, 6 Sections at 11 pm. These were report of day's operation. t Staff-Capt. Indian Cav. B.M.	Rain.
HEBUTERNE	Nov. 14th	8 am	At 4 am. Lieut O'CONNOR arrived at HQR with relief KDG under Sergt Colly, and 5 men from 29th Section with Supply Puran Singh — At 4:45 I took over forward guns at 4:45 am — and Lieut HOLT arrived at 5:30 am reporting relief completed and absence of injuries keen out. A quiet night —	

WAR DIARY
INTELLIGENCE SUMMARY

Place	Date	Hour	Summary of Events and Information	Remarks and references to Appendices
HEBUTERNE	Nov. 14.	8 p.m.	Alternate guns of each section were kept firing intermittently during the day on raid targets - at 8.30 a.m. Reinforcements under Jem^r. Mahabaleigh arrived from COIGNEUX. - During the night 92nd + 93rd BDes had been relieved by 94th BDe. All work kept red from Lieut O'Connor at 11 a.m. + 2 p.m. at 2.30 Lieut O'Connor wounded - at 4.45 p.m. sent men to Lieut O'Connor to bring all men and guns out - and report when all clear - sent carrying party of 12 additional men at 12.30 p.m. Captⁿ WINSLER had handed over command of combined group the and 93rd M.G. Coy. was relieved by 94th Coy. - At 7.30 p.m. new red from 3L Bivouar for 4th GARROT TRENCHED Squadⁿ return to COIGNEUX at rear. Immediately sent men to Sgt S. Arden + Lan Spadem transport at HEBUTERNE at 1 p.m. at 8.30 Lieut O'Connor had reported all clear from forward positions and left there his wound dressed - at 5.30 p.m. Enemy began Shell HEBUTERNS very heavily with 9.2. 5.9. and H.E. - Lieut HARRISON was detailed to supervise loading party - and through with transport with 10th 28th Section. N.C.O. Sect^{ns} thank at 1.45 p.m. under Lieut HOLT and Sgt. Sect^{ns} under Jem^r Mahan Singh at 2 a.m. - Enemy still shelling HEBUTERNE heavily - handed over Emplacements dump to O.C. 94th M.G. Coy -	Am.

WAR DIARY or INTELLIGENCE SUMMARY

Army Form C. 2118.

Place	Date	Hour	Summary of Events and Information	Remarks and references to Appendices
BOUCHAVESNES COIGNEUX	Nov. 15th	8 p.m.	Transport arrived at 1 a.m. and marched under Lieut HARRISON at 1.30 – at 2.15 a.m. LIEUT WARD reported left section shelters than previously inspected Right Sector – and at 2.30 a.m. with Lieut Ward & SSM Walsh started for COIGNEUX – all ranks in huts in COIGNEUX by 4 a.m. – 4.30 a.m. Rec'd orders from 13th Corps to report to 2nd Bgde Hqrs Fanshaws – at BETRANCOURT attres – phoned to G.S. XIII Corps – asking for 24 hours rest for the men – this was granted at 3 p.m. The Squadron was inspected by C.O.C. 2nd Bgde, and thanked for their work – and congratulated on their appearance after 25 days in the trenches – at 4 p.m. Jrode over to BETRANCOURT and reported to C.O.C. 2nd Bgde. Who's are allotted to the Squadron – and here received that the Sqdn would come under orders of C.O.C. 32nd Bgde in the 17th as 2nd Bgde was being relieved – sent in recommendations for immediate reward to XIII Corps – through Capt Hindles – Lieut Jollett JAR reported his arrival – horses ambulance –	Rain
BETRANCOURT	Nov. 16th	8 p.m.	The Squadron marched from COIGNEUX to BETRANCOURT at 2 p.m. – and were in billets by 5 p.m. reported to 2nd Bgde at 7.30 p.m. – had the arranged trench routes for morning of 17th.	Rain

WAR DIARY or INTELLIGENCE SUMMARY

Army Form C. 2118.

Place	Date	Hour	Summary of Events and Information	Remarks and references to Appendices
BETRANCOURT	Nov 17	8 pm	Maj-General Walker V.C. C.O.C. 2nd Div. inspected Judean Section at 9 a.m. and congratulated him on the work they had done and their appearance. At 2. p.m. reported to C.O.C. 32nd Brig. who showed us the area occupied by this Division in the Trenches, and returned here to reconnoitre the area at once. The day was spent by the men in cleaning kit & testing.	Rain
"	Nov 18	8 pm	Reported to I Corps HQ at ACHEUX - 9.30 - and to Lt Colonel Buchanan Corps Admin in M.G. & E. Corps - Lieut WARD + HARRISON reconnoitred from CHEEROH, ELLIS SQUARE, to WHITE CITY - and returned at 6.35 pm with full particulars.	Rain
"	Nov 19	8 pm	I left with Lieut WARD at 7.30 a.m. to complete reconnaissance of trenches reported to HQ 14th B.B. + HQ 97th B.B. in ELLIS SQUARE & WHITE CITY respectively, and also to O.C. 14th M.G. Coy. Reached Betris at 2.30 p.m. and found orders had been recd for Bn Section to proceed at once and report to C.O. 14th B.B. Lieut Harrison had rec'd orders to 2.36.5 I.A. Section and 1 A.S.C. Section were left to march at 3 pm. Lieut Harrison went forward immediately at 2.30 pm. and I ordered Lieut Follet to go up with the party at 3.10. Reported to Brig. Sect. All 3 Section had left for trenches.	

2449 Wt. W14957/M90 750,000 1/16 J.B.C. & A. Forms/C.2118/12.

WAR DIARY or INTELLIGENCE SUMMARY

Army Form C. 2118.

Place	Date	Hour	Summary of Events and Information	Remarks and references to Appendices
BETRANCOURT (advanced Happy Lines, Junction of B'd Ave & View Trench)	Apr 19th	8 p.m.	Sept Filters at 6.35 a.m. and proceeded to forward sections – found Lieut Harris was digging position for 4. 38" Guns in high ground near CHEEROH TRENCH – for night firing – These emplacements were complete by 4 p.m. and guns laid – orders were read to this allight. A German front line at half of 750 yards for harassing fire – No.I Lieut. Holt lickers ordered up to a position in Old German 2nd line many orders Capt. 1st DORSETS – this section left at 5.20 p.m. from ration dump – Buffs Chapman Singh 36th I.H. Killed – at 7.45 p.m. while in charge of this section – Lt HOLT and No.I section arrived back at 6th Avenue dug out at dawn – Very cold – and no corresponding orders for men – at 12.30 p.m. Lorried LIEUT WARD to where LIEUT HOLT and he arrived at 3.30 p.m. The same orders for 38th Section h: night firing – at 4.45 p.m. Lt WARD and No.I Sect's went to form covering party for a large working party digging accommodation trench from our old front line to German mined front – his return to heavy land – This party left ration dump at 5.30 p.m. enemy shelled our positions in CHEEROH – but no casualties.	Rain.
"	20th	8 p.m.		Rain.

Army Form C. 2118.

WAR DIARY
or
INTELLIGENCE SUMMARY

(Erase heading not required.)

Place	Date	Hour	Summary of Events and Information	Remarks and references to Appendices
6th Ave to View Trail & BETRENCOURT	21st	8 pm	Lt WARD with No. I. Section reached HQtrs dug out at dawn — they had been in action for 5 hours in left of working party, 200 yards from German line — no casualties — at 5 pm recd orders to concentrate at BETRENCOURT — Winters sent for — and all three sections were put in billets at BETRENCOURT by 8 pm. Reported at to OC 14th Bn — no further casualties —	Rain.
BETRENCOURT	22nd	8 pm	All ranks comfortable in billets — 32nd Divl Reinforcements — no change.	Rain.
"	23rd	8 pm	No change — baths arranged for all ranks —	
"	24th	8 pm	No change.	
"	25th	8 pm	No change — at 7.30 recd orders for whole squadron with transport to entrain at BELLE EGLISE at 8 a.m. 26th inst — orders for squadron to parade at 6 a.m. 26th inst —	
En route to WOINCOURT	26th	8 pm	The Squadron marched at 6 a.m. for BELLE EGLISE. LIEUT WARD - Transport under LIEUT FOLLETT - Reported accident to 7th Brits & Tan horses at 7 a.m. Commenced entraining at 9 a.m. all loaded by 10 a.m. Left BELLE EGLISE at 2 p.m.	Rain.

2449 Wt. W14957/M90 750,000 1/16 J.B.C. & A. Forms/C.2118/12.

Army Form C. 2118.

WAR DIARY
or
INTELLIGENCE SUMMARY
(Erase heading not required.)

Instructions regarding War Diaries and Intelligence Summaries are contained in F.S. Regs., Part II. and the Staff Manual respectively. Title Pages will be prepared in manuscript.

Place	Date	Hour	Summary of Events and Information	Remarks and references to Appendices
HYMMEVILLE	27th	8 p.m.	The Squadron arrived at WOINCOURT at 5.30 a.m. Entrainment all clear by 8.20 a.m. The men left in lorries for Squadron HdQrs - under Lieut WARD - Transport marched under Lieut POLLET and men MRs at 8.20 in 1st and Car.Bde. cars and reported arrival to O.C. Lucknow M.G. Squadron at HYMMEVILLE at 9.20 a.m. Squadron billetted as follows :- HQ in HYMMEVILLE; British tents CAMPAGNE (reckon). Sent QUESNOY Lieut Holt rejoined H.Q. & is attached as Staff Offr to the Squadron.	Appen.
"	28th	8 a.m.	Cleaning of Rifles & improving horse standings.	Nil.
"	29th	8 a.m.	G.O.C. LUCKNOW Cavalry Brigade inspected billets & congratulated the all ranks on their work. The Kentish Squadron employed in cleaning materials & improving standings	Nil.
"	30th	8 a.m.	Temp. Lieut Musson left for a six weeks course at the Cavalry Machine Gun Training Centre UCKFIELD. One out 29A Lance Sergt arrived from QUESNOY to FRIÈRES, to fur__ place being too crowded.	Nil.

[signature]
O.C. LUCKNOW M.G. Squadron

1/7/16

SERIAL NO. 316.

Confidential

War Diary

of

Machine Gun Squadron, Lucknow Cavalry Brigade.

FROM 1st December 1916 TO 31st December 1916.

No. 7

WAR DIARY,

OF

MACHINE GUN SQUADRON.

For the month of

DECEMBER, 1916.

==*=*=*

Army Form C. 2118.

WAR DIARY
or
INTELLIGENCE SUMMARY
(Erase heading not required.) LUCKNOW MACHINE GUN SQUADRON

DECEMBER 1916.

Place	Date	Hour	Summary of Events and Information	Remarks and references to Appendices
HJMMEVILLE	1 Dec	8 p.m.	Squadron preparing and to billets etc. & generally cleaning up & making good deficiencies. One Sect. 29th Lancers moved from QUESNOY LE FRIERE, the former village being overcrowded.	Yes
	2 Dec.	8 p.m.	No change	Yes.
	3 Dec.	8 p.m.	Divine service for the Squadron at Squadron HQ Quarters	Yes
	4 Dec.	8 p.m.	Commenced Squadron training in accordance with a scheme submitted to the Brigade.	Yes
	5 Dec.	8 p.m.	No change	
	6 Dec.	8 p.m.	no change	
	7 Dec.	8 p.m.	no change	Yes.
	8 Dec.	8 p.m.	no change	Yes
	9 Dec.	8 p.m.	no change	Yes
	10 Dec.	8 p.m.	no change	Yes
	11 Dec.	8 p.m.	no change	Yes
	12 Dec.	8 p.m.	no change	Yes
	13 Dec.	8 p.m.	no change	Yes
	14 Dec.	8 p.m.	no change	Yes

Army Form C. 2118.

WAR DIARY
or
INTELLIGENCE SUMMARY

(Erase heading not required.)

Instructions regarding War Diaries and Intelligence Summaries are contained in F. S. Regs., Part II. and the Staff Manual respectively. Title Pages will be prepared in manuscript.

64

Place	Date	Hour	Summary of Events and Information	Remarks and references to Appendices
HYMMEVILLE	15 Dec	8 p.m.	No change	
"	16 Dec	8 p.m.	Marching Order inspection by G.O.C. the Brigade in which it was pointed out that G.S.	
			No 6 carries a rifle the Range finder is little to become damaged.	
"	17th	8 p.m.	No change	
"	18th	8 p.m.	29th Sect at FRIERE moved into FRIEVILLES at 2.3 p.m. Munier in charge	
"	19th	8 p.m.	No change	
"	20th	8 p.m.	No change	
"	21st	8 p.m.	No change	
"	22nd	8 p.m.	No change	
"	23rd	8 p.m.	No change	
"	24th	8 p.m.	No change	
"	25th	8 a.m.	Christmas Day	
"	26th	8 p.m.	No change	
"	27th	8 p.m.	No change	

Army Form C. 2118.

WAR DIARY
or
INTELLIGENCE SUMMARY
(Erase heading not required.)

Place	Date	Hour	Summary of Events and Information	Remarks and references to Appendices
HYMMENUILLE	28th	6k-	No change	
	29th	8h.	Taken a new chitte for Machine Jun Structure. Thought it too confidential	Re
	30th	6h	Got more of the new chitte. G.O.C. Bde. present. a conference of the Machine Jun Structure Commanders of the 61 Cavalry Division in illet to discuss it & report on this new chitte	Ins
	31st	6h	No change	Re

J. Winchilff
O.C. Lucknow M.G. Squadron

2449 Wt. W14957/M90 750,000 1/16 J.B.C. & A. Forms/C.2118/12.

www.ingramcontent.com/pod-product-compliance
Lightning Source LLC
Chambersburg PA
CBHW081237170426
43191CB00034B/1964